CONQUERING CHAOS

by

Leo Calvin Price

Conquering Chaos
by Leo Calvin Price

Printed in the United States of America

ISBN 1-60034-506-9

Unless otherwise indicated, Bible quotations are taken from the King James version of the Bible.

www.xulonpress.com

Goods Best
Is yours

12.10.06

A NOTE FROM THE AUTHOR:

Chaos means that everything is out of control and it is growing exponentially. Sometimes life seems like a black hole and everything is being sucked in. You can't seem to get a grip on anything, you're sliding down a greased pole, a slippery slope and you can't find traction. You know what I mean When asked for a real life definition of Chaos, I was reminded of the Great Duke Ellington's definition of Rhythm: *"When you got it you don't need no definition and if you don't have it, ain't no definition gonna help."* Conquering Chaos will help you find traction and get a grip even when you can't define it.

Leo Calvin Price

BIOGRAPHY

Leo Calvin Price started ministry in 1963 and has served as a Senior Pastor and Associate Pastor. He is a graduate of a Southern Bible School and has traveled extensively around the world from Mexico to India. Leo has served his Faith by ministering in Men's Advances and churches with his unique ability to translate the power of the Christian life to individuals and churches. He has also served his Country in military service without reservation. One of his primary goals is to produce in individuals the knowledge that if one stands up on the inside they can stand up on the outside. He is recognized, by the churches that request his ministry, as one who has a unique giftedness to communicate and paint pictures with words which cause the reader to walk, feel and experience the blueprint for life that God has laid out before them. These pictures often remain and provide strength and encouragement to the listener. When the reader is finished, he or she will understand that they have been able to sense the depth of insight and the wisdom gleaned from life. Leo has lived his writings, from the death of his wife and unborn child in an auto accident to a broken relationship. Coming from the pain of self-inflicted emotional and intellectual isolation and learning how to hide in plain sight the reader will get rare glimpses of what happens when avoidance replaces acceptance. You will also discover that his belief in the Christ of Christianity isn't just imaginary or abstract but practical and imperative and essential to life.

CONTENTS

AN APPRECIATION

I shall never forget stepping into an acquaintance's office after returning from my mother's memorial service. It had been one of her final request for me to conduct that service. His words after stepping inside his office had a profound affect that dug their way into the visceral of my soul.

"Well, you're an orphan now" he said without a smile.

I hadn't suspected the allies in my soul that would prop themselves and connect with that remark; they were however drawn together like a magnet and galvanized. Inner turmoil found solidarity in those words.

I realized that there were thoughts and emotions that were opened with these words.

These thoughts and emotions had temporarily climbed into an old trunk in the attic of my soul, closed the door and stored themselves. All that was needed was someone just to open my personal Pandora's Box. The self destruct button had been push and I scramble to find the code to shut it off before implosion would occur.

It really wasn't his fault, however thoughtless and careless the remark he just hadn't lost anything of worth and value...... yet.

I felt like a *cosmic orphan*. I never knew that one could be a Christian and still feel...... and be as the words of an old song said, *"all by myself."*

However true friends step into your world when the rest of the world is stepping out of yours. I'm fortunate and blessed to have friends that don't mind stepping into my world even when it's *chaotic*. They have helped me in *Conquering Chaos*.

MORAL THEME

It is difficult at times to stand when everything about us says to quit. When life says it's to hard, give up. It is in these moments when your heart is beating so hard it feels as if it's coming through your chest, drawing the next breath becomes painful and you can hear yourself sweat. When your own hurts are the only sound in your ears and you deaf to every sound of hope, that's when you realize its do or die. So what do you do......? You remember...... that in order to stand up on the out side, you have to stand up on the inside.

2 Samuel 22:5 through 2 Samuel 22:20

(KJV) [5]When the waves of death compassed me, the floods of ungodly men made me afraid; [6]The sorrows of hell compassed me about; the snares of death prevented me; [7]In my distress I called upon the LORD, and cried to my God: and he did hear my voice out of his temple, and my cry *did enter* into his ears. [8]Then the earth shook and trembled; the foundations of heaven moved and shook, because he was wroth. [9]There went up a smoke out of his nostrils, and fire out of his mouth devoured: coals were kindled by it. [10]He bowed the heavens also, and came down; and darkness *was* under his feet. [11]And he rode upon a cherub, and did fly: and he was seen upon the wings of the wind. [12]And he made darkness pavilions round about him, dark waters, *and* thick clouds of the skies. [13]Through the brightness before him were coals of fire kindled. [14]The LORD thundered from heaven, and the most High uttered his voice. [15]And he sent out arrows, and scattered them; lightning, and discomfited them. [16]And the channels of the sea appeared, the foundations of the world were discovered, at the rebuking of the LORD, at the blast of the breath of his nostrils. [17]He sent from above, he took me; he drew me out of many waters; [18]He delivered me from my strong enemy, *and* from them that hated me: for they were too strong for me. [19]They prevented me in the day of my calamity: but the LORD was my stay. [20]He brought me forth also into a large place: **he delivered me, because he delighted in me.**

No matter how... resourceful any of us may be, we don't have the resources to be a redeemer.

Jack Hayford
A NEW TIME & PLACE

Chapter One

A PRIVATE AND PERSONAL HELL

'C', sat across the desk looking tense and stressed out. Just the pressure of being there was almost more than he could bear. There was for him an almost over-whelming urge to get up and leave. I don't mean just a casual exit but a full tilt run for the door.

He needed to be here and he had wanted to be here, he had made the arrangements to be here, however, here was not where he wanted to be now.

A little bead of sweat was creeping down the right side of his face by his temple, moving pass the hairline. It was just one drop. Nevertheless, he could feel it. He didn't want to wipe it away for fear I would notice. I watched as he raised his right hand moving ever so slowly. His arm must have felt like a ton as his thumb brushed away the drop.

I tried to make the moment easier as I said to 'C', *"I'm glad you came here."* It wasn't true, though I tried to make it sound as if I were pleased. I have had this conversation before, not completely or exactly like this, but in abbreviated versions. Some of what was about to be said I didn't want to hear. It was going to be ugly and distasteful. We both probably felt that we were damned if we did and damned if we don't.

I wondered as I digressed for a moment how much of me would I see and hear in his story of pain, sorrow and regret. I knew however, he wouldn't see it in my face or eyes. I had my game face on, you know, the mask we use as a shield. He couldn't see it… his pain and agony was blinding him.

I knew what he wanted. He wanted it all, just to go away, as if nothing had ever happened. He wanted it to be, just a dream. He wanted to scream, *"wake up, it's not real, it's only a dream."* It wasn't however a dream, it really happened and he was already awake.

That's the kind of private and personal hell that has had a lid on it for so long, that like a volcano the pressure had built up to such a point it was going to implode and then explode.

It's like a tsunami created by an earthquake. The shelves, the footings underneath have shifted and now nothing can stop it. It's going to roll over everything in its path.

Now here it is. I could see it coming.

'C', shifted in his chair uncomfortably, his mouth is dry, his muscles are taunt and the words come laboriously, *"I don't know what happen or why it happened."*

The hell of it is, you really do know what happened and why. Oh, you may have displaced what happened, moved the memories around so you wouldn't have to deal with them, but you know just the same. That's the reason your in your own private and personal hell.

Fyodor Dostoevsky, the Great Russian writer of the 1800's, in his novel *Notes From Underground* gives us a look at a private and personal hell. He starts out in the very beginning:

"I am a sick man... I am a wicked man... an unattractive man... I refuse to be treated out of wickedness... I will not, of course be able to explain to you precisely who is going to suffer in this case from my wickedness...

Dostoevsky confesses years later that he *"defaulted on his life through moral corruption in a corner."* He knew that we hurt not only ourselves but others get caught in the wake of an erupting *personal and private hell.* The more you read Dostoevsky, the more you'll understand that he knew about the political hell of his time during the nineteenth century, he also knew a private and personal hell.

Dostoyevsky was born October 30, 1821, in Moscow, Russia. It was the time of the Czar's, just before Lenin. Lenin was influenced by the writings of Marx. He should have been influenced by the writings of Dostoyevsky, because he didn't Lenin created a hell on earth for millions of people. Lenin had said decades later about the Great Russian writer Dostoyevsky, he is a *"superlatively bad"* writer.

By the way, I interject here, to tell you, so that you may remember as you read this book that voices determine your choices.

In 1848, Dostoyevsky joined a group of young intellectuals, led by Mikhail Petrashevsky, which met to discuss literary and political issues. In the reactionary political climate of mid-nineteenth-century Russia, the repressive Tsar Nicholas I, fearing the spread of revolutionary ideas, regarded the group as highly dangerous.

Such groups were illegal, and in April 1849, Dostoyevsky and 23 others the members of the so-called "Petrashevsky Circle" were arrested, and charged with subversion. Dostoyevsky and several of his associates were imprisoned and sentenced to death. As they were facing the firing squad, an imperial messenger arrived with the announcement that the Czar had commuted the death sentences to hard labor in Siberia.

While in prison, Dostoyevsky underwent a profound spiritual transformation. His intense study of the *New Testament*, the only book the prisoners were allowed to read, contributed to his rejection of his earlier liberal political views and led him to opposition to the growing atheistic sentiment of the times and the conviction that redemption is possible only through faith in Christ.

Dostoyevsky was released from the prison camp in 1854; however, he was forced to serve as a soldier in a Siberian garrison for an additional five years. The decade following, from 1860 to 1870 was tempestuous for Dostoyevsky, marked by severe financial problems and ill health.

Before finding a spiritual awaking, Dostoevsky sought for relief for his soul in external things. He discovered things won't get you out of hell. Things are only synthetic and temporary opiate.

> "I wished to stifle with external sensations all that was ceaselessly boiling up inside me."
>
> Fyodor Dostoevsky

Hello! Man do I understand that.

Fyodor found out what we all will find out sooner or later and that is, whether we're in Siberia as a kind of hell or in a hell that someone else has made for us or in a hell of

our making, without Christ, there is no out...
just hell.

Brennan Manning puts it into perspective
for all of us:

> When tragedy makes its unwelcome
> appearance and we are deaf to every-
> thing but the shriek of our own agony,
> when courage flies out the window
> and the world seems to be a hostile,
> menacing place, it is the hour of our
> own Gethsemane. No word, however
> sincere, offers any comfort or conso-
> lation. The night is bad. Our minds
> are numb, our hearts vacant, our
> nerves shattered. How will we make it
> through the night?

When the first part of *Notes From
Underground* came out in 1864 in the January
and April issues of *Epoch* magazine, the
censors cut out many parts of his *Notes From
Underground*. In a letter to his brother Mikhail
he writes:

> "Where I mocked at everything and
> sometimes blasphemed for form's
> sake... that is let pass; but where from

all this **I deduced the need of faith and Christ...** that is suppressed."

Again, in *Notes From Underground,* Fyodor writes;

In every man's memories there are such things as he will reveal not to everyone, but perhaps only to friends. There are also such as he will reveal not even to friends, but only to himself, and that in secret. Then, finally, there are such......
as a man is afraid to ...... reveal even to himself......

King David knew that God wants honesty in the soul of you. In the caves and canyons that only, you have trod. The places where no one has gone before or has been allow entry. The place where we have put an entry denial fixture, the place with an emotional lock.

It is here in this place of the soul where the *"truth will make you free."*

John 8:32 (KJV) [32]And ye shall know the truth, and the truth shall make you free.

It is here where David says that God wants truth to rebuild what hell hath destroyed, devoured, decimated and left nothing in its wake but ashes.

Psalm 51:6 (KJV) [6]Behold, thou desirest truth in the inward parts......

When people lack ownership of truth, they usually resist it even when it is in their best interest!

When, *"The truth is replaced by silence... the silence is a lie."*
Russian poet; *Yevgeny Yevtushenko*

While facing the truth seems at times to be frightening and painful, in reality it will be liberating and healing. The power of truth in our lives will enable us and will be a greater force for us than against us.

Anatoly (Natan) Sharansky was born in the Ukraine in 1948 and studied mathematics in Moscow. He worked as an English interpreter for the great Soviet physicist and dissident Andrei Sakharov, and himself became a champion of Soviet Jewry and a worker for human rights. Convicted in 1978 on trumped-up charges of treason and spying for the United States, Sharansky was sentenced to 13 years in prison. After years in the Siberian gulag, he was released in a U.S.-Soviet prisoner exchange in 1986 and moved to Israel, where he founded a political party promoting the acculturation of Soviet immigrants.

Anatoly Sharansky, a Russian Jew, is one of the current leaders for the state of Israel. A few years ago, he and his wife visited his native soil of Russia, where he had fought so hard for human rights and paid so dearly for his efforts with years of imprisonment. He asked the Russian authorities for permission to visit the Lefortovo Prison, in which he had been incarcerated for so long. They finally and reluctantly gave in to his persistent pressure. When Sharansky and his wife entered that tiny space where he had been kept, he turned to her and said, "This is where I finally found myself, all alone, with nothing to live for except what I firmly believed in."

From there he went to a cemetery and laid a wreath on the grave of the noted physicist Andrei Sakharov. Andrei Sakharov was a Soviet physicist who became regarded as the *father of the Soviet hydrogen bomb,* contributing perhaps more than anyone else to the military might of the USSR.

Gradually Sakharov became one of the regime's most courageous critics, a defender of human rights and democracy. He could not be silenced, and helped bring down one of history's most powerful dictatorships.

In a brief speech to the press, Sharansky said, "Mr. Sakharov put his mind to the cause of the nation in helping build the atomic bomb. However, before he died he made a defining speech. He said that for most of his life he had mistakenly assumed that the most powerful weapon in the world was the atomic bomb. Then he said, 'I have now discovered that the most powerful weapon in the world is not the bomb **but the truth**."

Without facing the truth and accepting the truth the only other alternative is… *living in hell.*

You'll know when you made your bed in hell. You'll be like the optimist in hell; *"I'm not here and it's not hot."*

You refuse to admit anything to your self.

It's called denial.

"Living out of the false self creates a compulsive desire to present a perfect image to the public so that everybody will admire us and nobody will know us."

Brennan Manning
The Rabbi's Heartbeat

David in the Old Testament knew it. He knew you can't hide from God or your self.

Psalm 139:8 (KJV)... if I make my bed in hell, behold, thou *art there.*

Most of us try to untangle the inside mess of our lives, alone, while at the same time struggle to look good on the outside. We deny that anything is falling apart. However just beneath the veneer, the façade, just below the epidermis, we're a mess. Moreover, when we try to fix it without any help from outside, we usually make things worse

I think that Helen Joy Gresham – Lewis, puts into perspective for me, what it feels like to live in a very private and personal hell. When she was near death and trying to describe how it felt, she would quote; *"Alone into the Alone."*

We are, however, not a lone, though that is how many of us feel.

Our emotional wounds are predisposed to disconnect, disorient, disassemble and dismantle us, causing us, in the worst-case scenario to feel un-named, and unclaimed.

We have been so severed and pulled apart emotionally, that we have feelings arising out of those emotions that we don't have it together intellectually. We end up creating mental gymnastics to avoid the wreck that is fast approaching. We create a foundation of nothingness and as the old cliché puts it, we find ourselves involved with, *"much ado about nothing."* We disguise and bury ourselves with busyness. It becomes the opium for our void and the morphine for our pain. We fill any contemplative moments with some sort of palliative, filler, denial. It's always just a placebo, a panacea…an excuse not to deal with it.

Those emotions become such a collage of thoughts that we feel our only belonging…is to some black hole in the universe that sucks the very life out of us. We feel orphaned in life and relegated to belonging to the cosmos.

Many of our wounds give us the feeling that we are orphan's, left alone to fend for ourselves in some dark abyss. We feel a need, an insatiable drive, a compelling…a longing for belonging.

We feel guilty that our lives have been so chaotic and linked with the knowledge that we have contributed sometimes knowingly and other times involuntarily, we tend to despair of a life force…something to keep us going.

We need connection, however we feel safer with a disconnection. We feel less vulnerable when we are disconnected. Connection seems most of the time to mean transparency and vulnerability. However vital to life… connection must be… still one must use caution and all the powers of observation that can be used in order to make the correct connection. Do not to connect with those who have decided to quit, give up and walk out.

One of my favorite stories is that of Winston Churchill. Sir Winston Churchill took three years getting through eighth grade because he had trouble learning English. It seems ironic that year's later Oxford University asked him to address its commencement exercises.

He arrived with his usual props. A cigar, a cane and a top hat accompanied Churchill wherever he went. As Churchill approached the podium, the crowd rose in appreciative applause. With unmatched dignity, he settled the crowd and stood confident before his admirers. Removing the cigar and carefully placing the top hat on the podium, Churchill gazed at his waiting audience. Authority rang in Churchill's voice as he shouted, "Never give up!"

Several seconds passed before he rose to his toes and repeated: "Never give up!" His words thundered in their ears. There was a deafening silence as Churchill reached for his hat and cigar, steadied himself with his cane and left the platform. His commencement address was finished.

If we connect to those whose intelligence is connected to their posterior, buttock, then we can only expect to be dumped on with their personal intake of life and considering the most clear picture this can conjure this is not something one would want to pursue.

So don't quit or give up, just change your hook up and things will start to look up.

I shall never forget a friend mine that had three beautiful sisters. I watched while through their lives they would date doctors, lawyers and Indian chiefs and then date the bottom of the barrel. Their father would say to them, *"Your going to fly around the flower and land on the garbage."* He was correct in his assessments of their final disposing of their soul mate choice. Granted it could have been that to whatever degree you want to put to it that he prophesied it, I believe however in the final analysis, it was their choice. Whatever the case one would want to make, that's where they ended.

Connection gives us significance and identity. If I'm a cosmic orphan, then the only connection will be with some inanimate object that has no life.

What really becomes alarming is, if I'm alienated enough, disconnected enough, disassociated enough, any sign of life will be terrifying.

When I feel cutoff, disconnected and disenfranchised, when I feel fearful and marred, when my vision is distorted and blurred and I can only see ugly in the mirror, I have to remind myself that God does not specialize in cosmetics, to cover up pain... He deals with issues.

Larry Crabb, noted psychologist, from his series Inside Out says, and I quote:

> *"God's desire to get down to the core of my being... where I wrestle with anger, where I fight sexual urges that shouldn't be there, where I feel distant from others, where there's depression I hide from everyone else...* **to get down to the real issues of life, and accomplish change from the inside out."**

Then Dr. Crabb reminds us that when:

> *Our insides scream with the pain of loneliness and rejection and failure. It hurts so much that we try to relieve the hurt through our own efforts-often by withdrawing from others so that they won't have the opportunity to disappoint us further. In every relationship, we try to keep from looking and feeling bad, from being embarrassed, from reliving old disappointments-in short, we strive to avoid pain. But feeling that pain is a first step...* **driving us to a new level of dependence of Christ."**

Yes, C's pain blinded him and my cleverly, construct mask hid me, making the saying true: *"none is so blind as he who will not see."* Eventually everything gets stripped away and your left with only two alternatives... deal with it or it will deal with you.

I like the Old Persian proverb that goes something like this:

He who knows not, and knows not that he knows not is a fool; shun him.

He who knows not, and knows that he knows not, is a child; teach him.

He who knows, and knows not that he knows, is asleep; wake him.

He who knows, and knows that he knows, is wise; follow him
I have been the fool... shun him.
I have been asleep... wake him.
However, never have I felt like a wise man... follow him.

There have been times in my life that I was terrified at the thought of anyone discovering where the interior journey of life had taken me. I felt as if I had been emotionally hijacked, someone had taken over the controls. I was so paralyzed that I couldn't hit the panic button. Someone or something was at the helm and I just couldn't seem to get the controls back.

We want a place like the movie; "Panic Room," with Jodie Foster, who is a 30-year-old divorced woman with her daughter played by Kristen Stewart who hide in a safe room from three burglars looking for a cache of money. We want a panic room, some kind of safe room to run into, to hide out, to disappear from view. The terror of the thought of discovery becomes so great we want to fall off the grid... where there's nothing to track us with, no phone, no credit cards, and no social security number. It's hard to be a hero if you feel like a zero. When you've been emotionally hijacked you know there's a crash coming... you just don't know when.

The most frightening thing about emotional hijacking is that in the end, you know, there's no one at the controls and I am left... as if I were... a floundering ship on the ocean of life with without a rudder.

James 1:6 (KJV) [6] ...... For he that wavereth is like a wave of the sea driven with the wind and tossed.

I have wondered about 'C' many times since we first met. I know that at times "C" felt as if his life was one catastrophic event after another. I remember my dad saying to me on occasions: *"You can take a horse to water, but you can't make him drink"* and then my dad would add, *"But if you put enough salt on his tongue you can make him thirsty."*

I wonder if I was ever able to get 'C' down to the water and then I wonder if I had at least made him thirsty.

The road home or the road back will take as long as the detours we make or find along the way, the stops along the way and the artificial things we use to sedate ourselves. When one uses the artificial, the fake, the false, to find peace you get conditioned to cheap solutions instead of profound and deep answers.

I continue to pray for "C".

Most of us live our lives in quiet
desperation.

Henry David Thoreau

Chapter Two

THE MISFITS

I t was late in the afternoon as I stood up from my desk and moved around to the window, the sun was going down and there was an amber glow beginning to spread across the cobalt blue sky. There was a longing inside the visceral of my being to be somewhere else. If I could just translate myself to somewhere devoid of thought and emotions, even for just a moment… alas it was not to be.

"A" had just left my office as I begin to rehearse and reflect our conversation. The image and reflection was still being held captive in my mind.

"A" hadn't been out of the military very long. He had served his country during the

Vietnam War and come home unscathed at least physically. He had been fortunate and had not seen combat but had served in a specialize unit. He had been grateful for that blessing.

There were rumblings however down inside of him that had been there before Vietnam and were still there now. Other wars that he had engaged in which he did see combat, that did leave him with scars. No, they were not military actions on foreign soil. They were *silent wars, inward conflicts and he was still bleeding from wounds not yet healed.* He was one of the *walking wounded.*

"A" at one point, paused and with a hurt and confused expression looked at me during our conversation and said; *"I just don't seem to fit in…'* he waited for a moment then added, *'anywhere."*

I was reminded of the movie 'The Misfits' with Clark Gable and Marilyn Monroe in 1961, gives us some hints of what misplaced affection, living in the shadows of the past and being lost in place is all about. After all that's what being a misfit is… 'lost in place.'

It's feeling out of sync, out of the rhythm, out of step, just a little behind, to little to late, a day late and a dollar short. You feel like your going up stream in a canoe without a paddle. You go to a party and nobody talks you. Your single and everybody else is married.

I understand and know the emotion and feelings of what being a misfit is about. I know that duck out of water feeling. It *quacks* me up. *(I'm sorry, I just couldn't let it pass)*

I have felt like a cosmic orphan. I didn't seem to fit in any scheme of things. I felt somehow disconnected to my present reality. I was being sucked into a black hole in the universe.

I would like to have been a bridge over troubled water, but I couldn't seem to find away to the other side, and eventually when I got there, it was the wrong river... not to mention the vicious, cold and un-caring troubled water.

I'm too short, too fat, too tall, too shinny, all at the same time and that's pretty hard to be if not down right impossible. But that's how I felt.

Ooops... late again... got a-hurry... isn't it the right day... I just can't seem to get it right.

Your stomachs in knots now, what shall I wear? Will I say the right things? I wonder if they'll like me?

OK, so now, I'm all dressed up and nowhere to go.

When you have that hellish feeling of being a misfit, it is *a very private and personal hell* you go through.

I was sitting in a sidewalk cafe in Manhattan, New York and began to take notice of how many people were using headphones. As I counted, I came to the conclusion that by my own count it was approximately a ratio of 1 out of 10 people with headphones. Could it be that it was just good music they wanted to hear? Maybe they were listening to a positive message being delivered by a motivational speaker. Were they bored or were they avoiding the world around them? To my observation, there was something in their eyes that said to me, *"I don't want any contact."*

I can understand this in the world we live. If there is fear of any kind, then contact with the thing we fear will make us avoid interaction. For most of us, it's better to avoid the thing we fear than to deal with it. It's easier on the emotional circuitry. There are so many ways to hide. We are good at camouflage. We are the masters of disguises. If I hide or avoid you, I don't have to express how I feel.

"Just leave me alone," seems to be the body language. *"Alone"* is what happens. That brings *"loneliness"* and that spells *"hurt, inner pain of rejection or don't get into my space... however I do want my rejection of you to be so subtle you can't identify it, hopefully that won't cause any kind of confrontation so don't look me in eye."*

You've kept it hidden, you've learned how to use the camouflage and the clown make up. You have the laughing down to a science. You have perfected the *invisible man* routine and you have learned how to shrug and wave it all off, as if to say, I am unaffected.

Jack Hayford, in his book *A New Time & Place* says it succinctly; *"Qualities such as availability, simplicity, and unaffectedness are difficult to come by. It is fear that makes us pretend, masquerade, play our people games, or flirt with insincerity."*

Down deep in the visceral, of your being, in the deepest hidden corner of your soul, your fighting to maintain some kind of decorum, respectability, some kind of semblance of a life, some kind of civility. In reality, however, your really dealing with three basic struggles in life.

The first is identity: *"Who am I?"*

The second is importance *"Do I matter?"*

The third is impact: *"What is my place in life?"*

C. S. Lewis in his book, *A GRIEF OBSERVED* gives a poignant and insightful answer to the dilemma of; who am I, do I matter and what is my place in life when he says we are "God's patients, not yet cured."

There's still hope. There's always hope.

We then create an *entry denial fixture,* a lock that denies access to anyone

What a paradox. A perfect image for everyone to know and admire us but no one knows who we are. We try to create a Utopian world for our perfect image to live in, when the reality is anything but... Utopian. So, we go deeper into the illusion and without realizing we make the pain greater, harder to heal and then consequently harder to conceal. After all that is really what we are trying to do. Hide in plain sight.

The poet John Donne (1572 – 1631) in his Meditation XVII address the issues that we are not alone, we are not isolated and that we will be faced with, at sometime our own mortality.

Perchance he for whom this bell tolls may be so ill, as that he knows not it tolls for him; and perchance I may think myself so much better than I am, as that they who are about me, and see my state, may have caused it to toll for me, and I know not that... all mankind is of one author, and is one volume; when one man dies, one chapter is not torn out of the book, but translated into a better language; and every chapter must be so translated; God employs several translators; some pieces are translated by age, some by sickness, some by war, some by justice; but God's hand is in every translation, and his hand shall bind up all our scattered leaves again for that library where every book shall lie open to one another. As therefore the bell that rings to a sermon calls not upon the preacher only, but upon the congregation to come, so this bell calls us all; but how much more me, who am brought so near the door by this sickness... No man is an island, entire of itself; every man is a piece of the continent, a part of the main... Any man's death diminishes me, because I am involved in mankind, and therefore never send to know for whom the bells tolls; it tolls for thee... Tribulation is treasure in the nature of it, but it is not current money in the use of it, except we get nearer and nearer our home, heaven, by it... If by this consideration of another's danger I take mine own into contemplation, and so secure myself, **by making my recourse to my God, who is our only security.**

We are all a part of the whole. "No man is an island." We always affect others by what we do in our living. Our current dominant thought is influenced by what we read, what we watch and to whom we listen. It only takes a little research to find the trail back to the point of origin of our current dominant thought. Follow the string or the crumbs back and you'll find out where it started, where it all began.

I often tell men when speaking to them either individually or at conferences and for that matter to anyone who has discovered that somebody is always watching and listening;

"Every man is a hero and an oracle to somebody, and that person, whatever he says has enhanced value."
                                        Ralph Waldo Emerson

When we look at the moral fiber, the hypocrisy, betrayal and greed and see the unsettledness that it brings, is it any wonder that people feel that something is out of order. Something doesn't fit.

You can scan the papers from the Wall Street Journal to the New York Times, from the Boston Globe to the L. A. Times and everything in between and find the drawn curtains of private lives that we thought were secure and happy only to find out when the curtain is lifted, their lives weren't so serene or controlled.

Taken collectively, the heedless lack of restraint in behavior reveals something disturbing about the moral character. We find ourselves wallowing in a moral morass. Ethics, is often dismissed as a prissy Sunday School word and when we do come to our senses in this human quagmire we find it is, likened unto the Prodigal Son in the canons *(an authoritative list of books accepted as Holy Scripture, the authentic works of a writer)* of the New

Testament writings of St. Luke. The Prodigal Son had so wasted his life that he was willing to settle for the husk of the pig pin. However the writer Luke says when the prodigal *"came to himself"* he ask himself, the very question we will ask ourselves; *"What am I doing here?"*

With such a chaotic jungle around us, finding spiritual direction is literally impossible with out God. There did you see that. I slipped that God thing in there.

Jonah 2:1 through Jonah 2:2 (KJV)
[1]Then Jonah prayed unto the LORD his God... [2]And said, I cried by reason of mine affliction unto the LORD, and he heard me; **out of the belly of hell cried I**, *and* thou heardest my voice.

Feeling like a misfit many times causes us to determine to do it our own way. Find our own way out. Find our own place in the sun. Find our own path to redemption. So we run here and we run there trying to find where we fit. To find out for what purpose we were designed. We tend to feel like the cartoon of the man pondering with the caption beneath it that read, *"I've been here and I've been there… but just one time I'd like to be where it's at."*

I wonder if "A" got the message I was trying to send. Much of it was the same message I tried to share with "C." However, something in both of their expression said the same thing… their pain deafened them to the resounding, reverberating answer.

I am reminded of Brennan Manning's words; "When tragedy makes its unwelcome appearance and we are deaf to everything but the shriek of our own agony, when courage flies out the window and the world seems to be a hostile, menacing place, it is the hour of our own Gethsemane. No word, however sincere, offers any comfort or consolation. The night is bad. Our minds are numb, our hearts vacant, our nerves shattered. How will we make it through the night?"

I know Christ is the answer. However, they don't know it and when the pain is greater than your ability to hear, then the answer is voiceless.

I spoke of trust, they were aquatinted and familiar with doubt. I spoke of faith they understood fear. I spoke of hope they thought it fantasy. I spoke of Christ they only knew crisis. I told them I knew, I told them I had been there… they had already left the building and yet hadn't left their chair.

I knew, I understood. I pray they will.

"Lord I believe, help thou my unbelief."

Late have I loved Thee, O Beauty so ancient and so new, late have I loved Thee! And behold, Thou wert within and I was without. I was looking for Thee out there, and I threw myself, deformed as I was, upon those well-formed things which Thou hast made. These things held me from Thee...Thou didst call and cry out and burst in upon my deafness; Thou didst shine forth and glow and drive away my blindness; Thou didst send forth Thy fragrance and I drew in my breath, and now I pant for Thee; I have tasted and now I hunger and thirst; Thou didst touch me, and I was inflamed with desire for Thy peace. When I shall cleave to Thee with all my being...my life will be alive, wholly filled with Thee.

St. Augustine

James 4:7 (KJV)
⁷Submit yourselves therefore to God.
Resist the devil, and he will flee from you.

Chapter Three

ONE DEGREE OF SEPERATION

"L" and his wife had been married for sometime… something and someone had come into the picture. Fame and fortune was enticing one, the want of a family for the other. Now in both or their faces was etched the pain of regret and chiseled in both was the look of *"I should have known better."*

I listened intensely as they both told their stories. As I listened, I found myself trying to concentrate, to distinguish between what they were telling me and the other painful stories I had heard through out the years. Without them noticing, I flinched inside... I had lived their story.

The faces were different, the geography was different, the immediate location was different, the voices were different, however the stories, the telling of the tale and the pain that came with the sound of their voices, I was becoming all to familiar.

Weddings are heavenly.

Divorces are hellish.

In weddings, everybody wins... in divorces, everybody looses... especially when there are children in the mix.

Ordinary people caught in extraordinary and sometimes bizarre circumstances, trying to explain the state of affairs.

By the time they arrived and sat down in front of me, I could see it was only a formality, an appeasement to family and friends. The decision had already been made. First blood had already been drawn.

In just a few days, he would come home from the office to any empty house. To a house so vacant that his footsteps would echo and sound as if, he were in a canyon. One day it's home... the day after it's a house... but the next day... ???

So close to having it all... now nothing.

Sometime latter I saw "L" and he told me that for years after our meeting his inner life had been a war of *'Conquering Chaos.'*

The *Conquering of the Chaos* of anger. Anger is always tough to manage. I think Aristotle said it best:

"Anyone can become angry that is easy. But to be angry with the right person, to the right degree, at he right time, for the right purpose, and in the right way... *this is not easy.*"

Anger can come out of unmet expectations, unfulfilled needs, fear, guilt, shame, stress. If these issues are not laid out, they will fester and simmer until they boil over. Many times, the issues have been hidden just below the surface for so long that they have lost their meaning but not their force and their potential for disaster.

Sometimes our anger prejudices us and makes us blind to Christ... and to His ability to help us.

The line between anger and answers is many times only one degree of separation.

Anger clouds judgment. Anger wants immediate response. Anger wants retribution. Anger wants justice and it wants it now.

Answers on the other hand, may mean waiting a moment to be able to see clearly. Wait for emotions to subside, to diminish. Answers may mean listening to another voice outside the one raging in your head. Answers may mean seeing a bigger picture.

Dr. George Woods puts this one degree of separation about anger and answers into perspective for us. While on a tour trip with his wife and friends, decided to read while they were traveling by bus to another location. After sometime of reading, Dr. Woods removed his glasses to rest his eyes. Upon returning his glasses to his eyes, he noticed his right eye blurry. Dr. Wood was immediately alarmed. After refocusing several times, he determined that he had been afflicted with a minor stroke. In an effort not to alarm his wife and friends, whom he knew would want him to seek immediate medical attention, stayed to himself through the lunchtime insisting his wife and friends continue to fellowship during lunch.

While contemplating his situation, he proceeded to be angry with himself, that he had allowed this to happen and angry with God for allowing this to take place.

At that moment, the tour guide came up and addressed Dr. Woods, *"Dr. Woods,* the tour guide said, *"I found the lens to the right side of your glasses."*

Sometimes just a step back, a different perspective, or a deep breath can make a difference. Sometimes there is only one degree of separation between anger and answers.

Then there is the ***Chaos*** of desire verses lust. Things can really get ugly in this melting pot of passions. Lust is desire distorted, perverted, altered and changed. Desire in its purest form is a God idea. Desire in its ugliest form is lust conceived by devilish influence. While desire develops, lust demands. Desire has conscience, lust is unconscionable, lust cares nothing about right or wrong. Desire produces care for the object pursued, lust demands control. Desire will surrender the heart, lust will have nothing less than immediate, self-centered and self-seeking gratification. Desire is self-less, lust is selfish.

The line between desire and lust is one degree of separation. That one degree of separation is call choice. Love is about giving. Lust is about taking. Love is about others.

Lust is about me. Love will guide you. Lust will drive you. You choose which one to whom you will surrender.

Then there is the ***Conquering of the Chaos*** of greed.

Some time ago there was a James Bond movie with the title; *'The World Is Not Enough.'* A wealthy man in America some years ago was ask how much wealth is enough and his response was *"just a little more."*

Our secular culture as well as our Christian culture sings the old song; *'Money, Money, Money.'* I know it's an old rock and roll song, but the band hasn't stop playing and we're still singing.

I will at my own risk venture to say that many of our television ministries have become info-commercials with a Christian slant, *(and oh by the way have you taken your vitamins today)*, as well as, *positive thinking* programs. Ok, sit up..., backs straight..., cross your legs and lets chant; *'everything's coming my way.'*

All right, so I'm in trouble. Anyway, just because it's not true for you and I, doesn't mean it's not true. Just because something's big doesn't mean it's better. Sometime less is more. I think, and this is just me thinking out

loud, *"I need Christ more than currency."*
Hey! I'm not knocking the currency thing.
We all have needs and wants, I guess I need
to work on knowing the difference between
need it and want it. I'm not saying we should
start singing a *'Billie Holiday'* song written
back in 1941, the theme however is still the
same, *'God Bless The Child.'*

Well the strong seem to get more
While the weak ones fade
Empty pockets don't ever make the grade

And when you got money
You got lots of friends
Crawling round your door

When the money's gone
And all your spending ends
They won't be around no more

Rich relations may give you
A crust of bread and such
You can help yourself but don't take too
much

'Cos Mama may have
Papa may have

But God bless the child that's got his own,
That's got his own

The motto for today is; I want my piece of the sky... now ... not in the by and by.

Anger, lust and greed are the great spoilers of our day. They must be discerned, discovered, destroyed and not rationalized or redesigned for acceptability. They must not become the primary priorities of our lives or the reason we live.

These elements create such universal disorder that chaos is the only deductive conclusion. They will affect everything from social disorder to emotional as well as physical breakdown.

My dad was a believer in earning respect. What we don't earn or appreciate we usually spurn, disdain or have no respect. In essence, we are not grateful or thankful for what we have. I know this is not a hard fast rule. However, I do believe it to be true. In everything my dad worked on the issue was not about greed, it was about earning respect.

My dad would to tell me when we were about to start a difficult task or project and, or, if we were already involved in a project and by the way, the task or project was in reality going to be work… dad would say… "This will separate the men from the boys." The statement was full of all kinds of underlying suggestions, such as "finish what you start" and "if the job is worth doing it's worth doing right." However, his main thought was, this will separate those who can from those who can't. It was about earning respect on a job well done. Not cutting corners for a cheap dollar. Sometimes the difference between I can and I can't is *one degree of separation between a greed or time honored respect..*

What separates us is the choices we make and the motive behind those choices. It's the why that God looks at. Not what you say your motive is but what really is the reason your doing what your doing and asking what your asking for. I'm easily fooled, God isn't. Lets see… ummmm… what was it that the writer James said in the New Testament?

James 2:17 (KJV) [17]Even so faith, if it hath not works, is dead, being alone.

Having faith is tough and takes effort on our part. That effort is called worked. A minister friend of mine used to say that faith was spelled w-o-r-k.

Sometime ago there was a song that went something like this, "So close but yet so far away." Except for a few of the changes, that song could be any of us during our lives. We were so close to winning, on the brink of success and many times on the edge of failure. In most cases, the narrow, thin line between success and failure was only, *"One Degree of Separation."*

Many of our hopes, dreams and ambitions were within reach, just a touch away. You could feel success in your grasp, on your fingertips and then suddenly it was gone, like sand slipping through you fingers.

One Degree of Separation, sometimes is the only thing that stands between winning and losing.

What separates us?

Where is that point of no return?

What is that *"One Degree of Separation?"*

Where is the point, that line, that *one degree of separation* between faith and fear, love and hate, trust and doubt, peace and chaos.

Is it faith?

Is it the fickle finger of fate?

Is it the luck of the draw?

If we don't know, or if we don't care or if we don't find out, we will be left to the winds of adversity, to flounder on the burning sands of frustration or adrift on a sea of perplexity.

We will be in a constant state of flux, instability and there will continue to be the perpetual existence of doubt.

If we don't find out the difference between faith and fate, our lives will hinge on chance, the flip of the coin or on a deliberate choice based on whatever it is that we trust.

Living in the dark without God's help is like playing Russian roulette, once the cylinder has been spun you don't know which chamber has the bullet in it… *"round and round she goes, where she stops nobody knows."* Without God, it's a trapeze act without a net.

Faith is full of promise and hope, *(favorable expectation)*. However, fate has nothing but frustration to offer as its reward for following its lead.

Hope is the driving force to Faith. Hope sees the un-possessed. Hope says it's there. Faith says you can reach it. Hope visualizes. Faith actualizes.

Sometimes we dig for the treasure only to stop short. One more turn of the shovel was all it would have taken to change everything.

To change the winds of frustration...

To change being adrift on a sea of perplexity...

To change the constant state of flux and perpetual doubt... put the shovel in one more time and turn the blade.

I remember a story that comes to mind from years ago. As the story goes, a man had discovered a pearl of great price. However to purchase it he would have to sell everything that he possessed and travel a great distance. He sold everything he had and purchased the pearl. Returning on a ship and leaning against the rail reflecting his accomplishments, he pulls out the treasure. Admiring his magnificent achievement and in a moment of extreme excitement he tosses the pearl into the air. At that very moment, the ship lurches and the pearl falls unhindered between his fingers.

Everything he has falls into the ocean. He has lost *"the pearl of great price."*

Sometimes the words; "Lets face it... it can't be done or let's face it... you can't do it," becomes the challenge that puts us into the, "I can mode" or we cringe in terror because we have already determined, "we can't." We must be careful we don't become our own prophets of doom and despair.

We must be careful that the fear of losing is not greater than the desire to win.

Boris Becker the three-time winner of Wimbledon and the youngest champion ever made this remarkable statement;

"I drew my strength from fear.
Fear of losing.
I don't remember the games I won only the games I lost.

It seems that our culture is becoming a culture based on compromise. The reason, rivers are crooked is because they take the path of least resistance.

I'm reminded of the story of the man and his wife who are having dinner.

The husband and wife were having a fine dining experience at their exclusive country club when this stunning young woman comes over to their table, gives the husband a big kiss, says she'll see him later and walks away.

His wife glares at him and says, "Who was that?"

"Oh," replies the husband, "she's my mistress."

"Well that's the last straw," says the wife. "I've had enough, I want a divorce. I am going to hire the most aggressive, meanest divorce lawyer I can find and make your life miserable."

"I can understand that," replies her husband, "but remember, if we get a divorce it will mean no more wintering in Key West, or the Caribbean, no more summers in Tuscany, no more Cadillac STS in the garage, and no more country club, and we'll have to sell the 26-room house and move to two smaller homes, but the decision is yours."

Just then, a mutual friend enters the restaurant with a gorgeous young woman on his arm.

"Who's that with Jim?" asks the wife.

"That's his mistress," says her husband.

She replies, "ours is prettier.'

That's compromise in its most telling form.

Several years ago, financier Ivan Boesky openly described *greed* as "a good thing" while speaking at UCLA's business school.

That flawed thinking soon got him in trouble. When his unethical practices on Wall Street came to light, he was fined millions of dollars and sent to jail.

Ivan may have tapped into what he thought was a nerve running through our culture... but what he found was, eventually there will be a, *"nerve ending."* Excuse the play on words but I just couldn't help myself.

Greed is a compromise and offence to ethics not to mention truth and honesty. Sometimes individuals think because they are corrupt that everyone else in like them.

I have heard people say, *"lets face it we are all corrupt."* That may be true however I believe it only to be true to a degree and it's only true to the degree that much of this thinking depends on how one was raised and the character of that background, and, or what one chooses to buy into philosophically.

That does not mean that we yield to a corrupt thought or buy into *it, (it, being greed or anything resembling this framework.)* Just because it seems feasible within ones circle of reason...not buying into this...is called resistance. This is what separates the men from the boys...the weak from the strong...resistance.

Resistance is the first line of defense when it comes to compromise.

There's an old saying that goes,

"If you do what you've always done,
You'll get what you always got."

Some time ago, I was staying at a friend's house. In the evening, I would go for a five-mile run and watch the sun go down behind the mountains and feel the temperature change, as the sun would set.

About the same time I would head out for my run a man on a bicycle would ride his bike past the entrance where was staying. As was my regime, I would take time to stretch and watch, as he would ride by me several times before I left the complex. This scenario never changed.

As I ran outside the gates along the running and biking path I thought how strange it was that this man never left the community. He was not able to see the landscaping, the flowers or the full view of the mountains along the trail or meet with the other people who were either running, walking or riding their bikes. For him the scenery never changed.

Perhaps something bad had happened to him on some occasion out side the walls. I'm sure he felt safer and felt that he had better security for himself. Nevertheless, the scenery never changed.

Maybe it was safer inside the complex rather than outside. However, he never saw anything different.

This story may not be appreciated as a great analogy, however it spoke volumes to me. I was glad I was outside the wall. The trail was always different. The people, birds, the sun as it rises and sunset, life is always better outside…, our prison of pandemonium, outside the walls of our emotional wreckage, outside the walls of our confined chaos.

Sometimes it's not so much, what one lays down in life, as it is what one takes up in life.

What directs us? What is the life compass in our lives, that moral code, the principle over programs, this discovery is what gives us our true north.

Let's face it…Herman C. Weber's thoughts, in his 1931 book, on Evangelism parallels and puts into perspective our Christian culture. It sounds frightfully like our secular culture of today. We have successfully created a culture of;

- Policies without Principles...win at any price.
- Wealth without work...at the price of someone else.
- Pleasure without conscience...not my brother's keeper.
- Knowledge without character... accomplished crooks.
- Business without morality...every man for himself.
- Science without humanity...modern instruments of war.
- Worship without sacrifice...lip service.

Policies are many,
Principles are few,
Policies will change,
Principles never do.

For me the scary thought is how easy it seems for some *professing Christians especially* to be able, so easily, to step through and into the inferior, subjacent nether world and leap into the great abyss to the nothingness of lust, greed, avarice, anger and all that comes with just stepping over the line, *"the one degree of separation."*

The words of the great scientist, Albert Einstein, made this pungent statement: *"The splitting of the atom, has changed everything, save how we think.* Thus, he observed, *we drift toward unparalleled catastrophe."*

There in lies some of the problem. We tend to drift. My dad had an old saying; *"They were as pure as the driven snow, until they drifted."* I have discovered in traveling around the world, one must pay attention to driving or you can drift into on coming traffic. When that happens, turn out the lights.

Adversities will come. They must, because they reveal who we are.

Adversities do not make the man either weak or strong. They reveal what he is.

Several years ago, I heard of the Northwest Cod fish. Some time ago in the NW part of the United States, the fishermen ran into a problem with their Codfish. The problem was with the distribution. First, they had so many Cod that they built freezers to store them. However, it wasn't long until they discovered that the Cod lost their flavor quickly.

Then they decided to put them in salt water and ship them. The Cod just lay in the salt water, but by the time they arrived, the Cod had again lost their flavor.

Then they discovered the answer. Catfish are the natural enemy of the Cod. The fishermen then put Catfish in the shipping tanks. This caused the Cod to keep moving in the tank. When the Cod arrive and were prepared, they didn't lose their flavor.

Adversity will give you a *flavor (I just couldn't resist the pun)* of who, you are. I tell people all the time, including myself; *"If you don't stand up on the inside, you will never stand up on the outside."*

"L" and his wife never were reconciled. I would like to have been able to tell you that everything worked out and they found new life in the marriage, that didn't happen. What did happen is that they both moved on and ***Conquered the Chaos.***

I still pray for both of them.

If you can find a path with no obstacles,
it probably doesn't lead anywhere.

Frank A. Clark

Chapter Four

UNREALISTIC EXPECTATIONS

"V" had just met someone after his divorce, "it's like a dream come true" he exclaimed. Then those words that make your sonar start beeping came to my ears, "she's just what I prayed for."

"Great," I said, "so tell me what you prayed for." As he proceeded to tell me all the criteria he had ask for, the color of hair, height, look and personality. How was I going to respond? What was I going to say to answered prayer? The words started pounding in my inner ear, *"devil with a blue dress, blue dress, blue dress, devil with a blue dress on."*

I've often wondered why it is that we never consider that the enemy of our souls listens while we pray.

This answered prayer would eventually find it's answered source from hell.

No matter how I tried to suggest to him other things to pray about, he was already blinded by the light. Oh, she had everything he prayed for **and then some**. There in were hid the problems to come. He thought that the hair, look and personality were all that he needed. He never heard the other shoe drop until it was to late. He never did get the number of the Mac truck that hit him. He never heard the train from hell coming, I guess you'd have to realize you were on the tracks first. He just never saw any of it coming.

I'm reminded of the story of the gambler who listens to the little voice who says, "Bet on 28" so he does and wins, the voices says again, "bet on 34" so he does and wins again. Then the little voice says, "bet it all on 68" he does and loses everything... the little voice says, "Oooops."

The little voice said more than "oooops" to "V" it was to late then. It was all over but the weeping and the crying. The little voice was drowned out by his own voice with such disparaging, reproachable remarks like *"dummy, what's wrong with you, are you that stupid."* You can imagine the rest. I think Brennan Manning said it best:

> When tragedy makes its unwelcome appearance and we are deaf to everything but the shriek of our own agony, when courage flies out the window and the world seems to be a hostile, menacing place... No word, however sincere, offers any comfort or consolation. The night is bad. Our minds are numb, our hearts vacant, our nerves shattered. How will we make it...?

Don't get me wrong. I believe in praying to receive from the Lord. I have discovered however, God doesn't always give you what you want when He knows what you need. The devil however will give you what you want to stop you from getting what you need.

My point here is about unrealistic expectations. Don't blame God when you don't get what was best. You're the one that settled for the next best. Next nothing!!!!! You wanted what you wanted, when you wanted it and when it crossed your path, in your piousness, you thanked God, then went on your merry way. God said, *"why thank me, for what, I didn't give that to you."*

We all have the same proclivities, the same propensities to want it our way. Life however isn't Burger King, you can't always *"have it your way."*

The 18th Century British statesman Edmund Burke said it well:

> *"All men that
> are ruined are
> ruined on the side
> of their natural
> propensities."*

Much of our personal chaos comes from our propensity for unrealistic expectations. For instance, your not going to be able to afford a luxury home on the Southern California coast on $150.00 a week income. The Dilbert cartoon reminds me of people I've met:

> Pet dog to Dilbert, "I'm going to try my paw at being a career counselor. Insecure people will seek my advice and I'll tell them to be more self-reliant".

Dilbert responds to his pet, "That sounds lazy and unhelpful."

Dog's response, "would you want career advice from somebody who has to work hard?"

Your chances of winning the lottery are one in who knows how many millions. Unrealistic expectations. Hello!!!!!!!

I love the story of the man who prayed every day to win the lottery. Day after day, Bernie prayed. Finally God spoke and said; *"look Bernie, help out, at least buy a ticket."*

I'M NOT ADVOCATING BUYING A LOTTERY TICKET. IT WAS JUST A STORY, AN ATTEMPT AT HUMOR.

Depending on the background of your family or the lack thereof, or of a fantasy induced life produced by to much TV and too many movies, or of a Utopian existence that may have been created by the *"the have your way"* culture, that kind of inductive reasoning will eventually assume and conclude that, *"nothing will ever go wrong."* Let me warn you now that just a little bit of life will take care of that fantasy. There will never be enough money or power in this world to make it all right.

In the Peanuts comic strip, Charlie Brown ask, *"Which do you think lasts longer in life, the good things or bad things?"*

Linus replies, *"Good things last eight seconds, bad things last three weeks."*

Charlie Brown, *"What about in between?"*

Snoopy lying down on top of his doghouse says, *"In between you should take a nap."*

There are no naps for us. We have to pick up and start going again. There's no riding off into the sunset. We don't grab the money and run.

We know that there's no free lunch. We know that sex is never casual and drugs are not recreational. We have discovered responsibilities that make us stay the course.

Movies, television, magazines as well as many books paint unrealistic pictures that should we buy into their philosophies will cause us frustration and despair. There are no unattractive people in any of these mediums.

Hollywood and MTV will never get it, they will never understand the moral implication that they portray, nor do I believe that they want to know. They have bought their own press. They are only interested in pulling everyone they can into their own morass, jungle and chaos.

What I have just said about Hollywood, its agenda and to its political arena was put into perspective some years ago in Kansas State Legislature, Topeka on January 23, 1996. Pastor Joe Wright of Wichita's Central Christian Church was invited to deliver the invocation.

"Heavenly Father, we come before you today to ask Your forgiveness and to seek Your direction and guidance. We know Your word says 'Woe to those who call evil' good but that is exactly what we have done.

- We have lost our spiritual equilibrium and inverted our values.
- We confess that we have ridiculed the absolute truth of Your word in the name of moral pluralism.
- We have worshiped other gods and called it 'multiculturalism.'

- We have endorsed perversion and called it 'an alternative lifestyle.'
- We have exploited the poor and called it 'lottery.'
- We have neglected the needy and called it 'self-preservation.'
- We have rewarded laziness and called it 'welfare.'
- In the name of 'choice,' we have killed our unborn.
- In the name of 'right to life,' we have killed abortionists.
- We have neglected to discipline our children and called it 'building esteem.'
- We have abused power and called it 'political savvy.'
- We've coveted our neighbors' possessions and called it 'taxes.'
- We've polluted the air with profanity and pornography, and called it 'freedom of expression.'
- We've ridiculed the time-honored values of our forefathers and called it 'enlightenment.'

Search us, oh God, and know our hearts today. Try us, and show us any wickedness in us. Cleanse us from every sin, and set us free. Guide and bless these men and women who have been sent here by the people of Kansas and who have been ordained by You to govern this great state. Grant them Your wisdom to rule and may their decisions direct us to the center of Your of Your will. I ask it in the name of Your son, the living savior, Jesus Christ. Amen."

"V" didn't get what he prayed for... he got what he bargained for. He didn't ask what God wanted for his life, he told God what he wanted and just figured God would accommodate and acquiesce to his whims. We would do well to remember that God sometimes allows some things He does not purpose.

"V" wasn't going to ask God to search his heart and reveal his motive that would spoil the party he was going to throw. To bad the party threw him... if you get my drift. Lets see what was that song in the 60's, *"It's my party and I'll cry if I want to... cry if I want to... you'd cry to if it happened to you."*

Excluding God from the equation is always costly and painful. Remember: *sin will always take you farther than you wanted to go... keep you longer than you wanted to stay... and cost you more than you wanted to pay.*

It's the price of self-indulgence, self-reliance and the false pride of self-sufficiency. We want to look back and sing the song: *"I did it my way."* So you went down the primrose path of self-assuredness.

Failure isn't so bad if it doesn't
attack the heart.
Success is all right if it doesn't
go to the head.

Grantland Rice

Chapter Five

ENTITLED

"I deserve some happiness, don't I?"
"I'm entitled."
*"I thought it was my turn and my
time."*
"What happened?"
"Life just isn't fair."

"I" spoke with what seemed to me
as indignant anger that resonated
with resentment. His jaws taunt, his eyes
narrow slits and seemed to narrow with every
word, daring me to answer. His posture, with
his head set deep into his neck and his body
ridged was challenging me to come up with

the correct answer or there would be hell to pay.

I wanted to say; "hey, lighten up, I'm not the who or the what, that's made you unhappy and if there's hell to pay, the bills in your hand and I didn't give it to you." But I didn't.

Since, however I'm not a Psychologist, psychotherapist or a counselor and since I don't deal in past life regression therapy, incidentally I don't believe in it anyway, I can share these random thoughts with you.

Clairvoyance is not my strong suit, neither is reading tealeaves, and other than God speaking out of a burning bush, I'm going to need a lot more information. Things like, what is your definition of happiness, because invariably happiness means different things to different people. Most have concluded that acquisitions and attainments will make you happy. Not so. If you allow unhappiness, it will build a pool in your back yard so you won't have to go far to drown.

Unhappiness will ravage your soul and leave you if you survive adrift, alone and insecure. If you feel entitled, if you think happiness is your right, that life owes you, you've got a big surprise coming.

Happiness really is a choice. The dismantling of that choice is determined in terms of how resolute one may be in walking and working out that choice, to be happy.

Ravi Zacharais from his book *Jesus Among Other Gods* tells a story that emphasis this point;

I recall, in one of New York's leading newspapers, an interview with the wife of a New York Yankees ballplayer who had just signed $89 million contract. He had held out for a long while before signing, hoping that the management would match the $91 million offer of another team. The Yankees did not budge. His wife later said, *"When I saw him walk in the house, I immediately knew that he had not succeeded in persuading them to move up from eighty-nine million. He felt so rejected. It was one of the saddest days of our lives."*

That scenario will probably not be played out in most of our lives. It does however give us some insight to what lights up and determines much unhappiness in our lives. The two point spread between $89 million and $91 million, the points being a million each, does make it some what hard to grasp the, *"It was one of the saddest days of our lives."*

Yet many of us have the same battle on a far lesser scale and it's not always about money. It could be a position, a promotion or a person that we have somehow considered ourselves deserving of.

Wasn't I entitled?

Sometimes what we feel we deserve and what we get are two entirely different things.

Winston Churchill once said, *"It is not enough that we do our best; sometimes we have to do what's required."*

It seems much of our pain comes from unrealistic expectations.

I love the story that John Maxwell tells in his book, *'Failing Forward.* 'It's about the author of the *Three Musketeers* by Alexandre Dumas.

The novelist and a friend had a heated argument, and one challenged the other to a duel. Both Dumas and his friend were expert marksmen, and they feared that if they proceeded with the duel, both would die.

So they decided to draw straws to determine which of them would shoot him self. Dumas picked the short straw. With a sigh, he picked up his pistol, walked into the library, and closed the door, leaving behind him a group of worried friends.

After a few moments, the loud report of a pistol shot echoed from the library. His friends immediately charged into the room, and there stood Dumas with the pistol still smoking in his hand.

"An amazing thing just happened," said Dumas. "I missed."

It was un-realistic to think that he would shoot him self. Just like it would be un-realistic to think you could buy a million dollar home on a $150 dollars a week or even maintain it or expect someone to love you whom you never met.

Oscar Wilde the acclaimed British writer once said, *"In this world there are only two tragedies. One is not getting what one wants, and the other is getting it."*

The pain and aloneness that come from un-realistic expectations should cause one to examine that the pain may not be a lack of affection, but perhaps direction. Most of us want change; however we want it in somebody else. I love the Peanuts comic strip that puts this thought into perspective for us.

Lucy is leaning against a fence with Charlie Brown. *"I would like to change the world,"* she says.

Charlie Brown asked, *"Where would you start?*

She replied, *"I would start with you!"*

I remember a line from the movie *"Unforgiven"* with Clint Eastwood. Gene Hackman *'Little Bill'* is laying wounded on the saloon floor wounded, he looks up at Clint who's about to shoot him and end his life. Gene Hackman says something along the line, *'I don't deserve to die like this'* to which Clint says, *'deservin's got nothing to do with it.'*

Sometimes life is unfair. You thought you had the world in the palm of your hand and some how it slipped through your fingers. You're not alone. There have been many people who had it and lost and some were never even close, but most have continued on and persevered and kept trying.

Chris Nolan a paraplegic wrote *'Under The Eye Of The Clock.'*

Many of the *Psalms of David* were born in difficulty.

Most of the *Epistles of Paul* were written in prison.

Paul Bunyan wrote *Pilgram's Progress* from jail.

Booker T. Washington, George Washington Carver and Martin Luther King, Jr. succeeded in the face of racial discrimination.

So life isn't easy. It doesn't always go as you planned. Rodney Dangerfield probably expressed our feelings and said it best for most of us *'I don't get no respect.'*

Consider this. Who would crucify a man for telling people to love one another... pray for one another... help a neighbor in need... go the extra mile... feed the hungry... clothe the naked, crucifying a man like that wouldn't be fair would it. But it happened anyway.

Philip Yancey in his book, *'Disappointment with God'* that in the Hindu doctrine of Karma, which applies a mathematical precision to this belief, of unfairness, calculates it may take a soul 6,800,000 incarnations to realize perfect justice. At the end of all those incarnations, a person will have experienced exactly the amount of pain and pleasure that he or she deserves.

That thought exhaust me just thinking about it.

However along with Philip Yancey I believe there is something else. Maybe when we get out of our self indulgence, self absorption, with making things right for me, maybe just maybe, by helping someone else I can better help my own life. That however will be very hard to do if I'm so self involved that I can't see anyone else.

If I is the center of my universe the chances of my missing the traitor within, the self centered little voice will circumvent everything else in my life, to appease itself. If I allow the traitor of self serving, narcissism direct and dominate me at the expense of others then the castle wall has been breached from within.

The words of John Owen, from *Sin and Temptation* come to mind of my own seemingly self requirement that will in the end betray me for the lack of satisfaction.

"However strong a castle may be, if a treacherous party resides inside (ready to betray at the first opportunity possible), the castle cannot be kept safe from the enemy. Traitors occupy our own hearts, ready to side with every temptation and to surrender to them all."

When we feel entitled, we are saying I don't have to earn this or that I don't have to put some effort in but because I'm here I should have it. And when we don't get it, we feel life is unfair.

Ben Franklin once said; "There are three things extremely hard: steel, a diamond, and to know one's self."

It's amazing how it is that what we want today we may not want tomorrow. That comes from not knowing many time ones self. So it we don't have it now we feel cheated out of what we felt we were entitled to and therefore life is unfair.

There looms over us that thought that God doesn't love me like He love someone else. We forget that He gave His only begotten son, Jesus for all of us collectively and for us individually.

Whenever I'm tempted to think I'm entitled or that life is unfair I read the story of Kathy, from the book *'Cries Of The Heart'* by Ravi Zacharias.

KATHY – from the book Cries Of The Heart - RAVI

Some months ago I received a copy of a mailing from a ministry in New York City that works with young people who are trapped in the drug scene and often caught in the hellish web of prostitution. I cannot recall when a few words from a stranger left such heaviness within my heart. Prior to the salutation the writer warned the reader that it would be difficult to believe the contents but vowed that every word of it was true. Here is the text of that letter:

Dear Friend,

She came to our front door Tuesday morning, dressed in dirty rags, holding a little aluminum paint can in her arms.

From the second she stepped inside our shelter, she mystified us. Whatever she did, wherever she went, the paint can never left her hands.

When Kathy sat in the crisis shelter, the can sat in her arms. She took the can with her to the cafeteria that first morning she ate, and to bed with her that first night she slept.

When she stepped into the shower, the can was only a few feet away. When the tiny homeless girl dressed, the can rested alongside her feet.

"I'm sorry, this is mine," she told our counselors, whenever we asked her about it. "This can, belongs to me."

"Do you want to tell me what's in it, Kathy?" I'd ask her. "Um, not today" she said, "not today."

When Kathy was sad or angry or hurt-which happened a lot she took her paint can to a quiet dorm room on the 3rd floor. Many times on Tuesday and Wednesday and Thursday, I'd pass her room, and watch her rock gently back and forth, the can in her arms. Sometimes she'd talk to the paint can in low whispers.

I've been around troubled kids all my life . . . . I'm used to seeing them carry stuffed animals (some of the roughest, toughest kids at Covenant House have a stuffed animal). Every kid has something-needs something – to hold.

But a paint can? I could feel alarm bells ringing in my head.

Early this morning, I decided to "accidentally" run into her again. "Would you like to join me for breakfast?" I said. "That would be great," she said.

For a few minutes, we sat in a corner of our cafeteria, talking quietly over the din of 150 ravenous homeless kids. Then I took a deep breath, and plunged into it. . . .

"Kathy, that's a really nice can. What's in It?"

For a long time, Kathy didn't answer. She rocked back and Forth, her hair swaying across her shoulders. Then she looked over - it me, tears in her eyes.

"It's my mother," she said.

"Oh," I said. "What do you mean, it's your mother?" I asked. "It's my mother's ashes," she said. "I went and got them from the funeral home. See, I even asked them to put a label right here on the side. It has her name on it."

Kathy held the can up before my eyes. A little label on the side chronicled all that remained of her mother: date of birth, date of death, name. That was it. Then Kathy pulled the can close, hugged it.

"I never really knew my mother, Sister," Kathy told me. "I mean, she threw me in the garbage two days after I was born." (We checked Kathy's story. Sure enough the year

Kathy was born, the New York newspapers ran a story saying that police had found a little infant girl in a dumpster ... and yes, it was two days after Kathy was born.)

"I ended up living in a lot of foster homes, mad at my mother," Kathy said. "But then, I decided I was going to find her. I got lucky-someone knew where she was living. I went to her house."

"She wasn't there, Sister," she said. "My mother was in the hospital. She had AIDS. She was dying."

"I went to the hospital, and I got to meet her the day before she died. My mother told me she loved me, Sister," Kathy said crying. "She told me she loved me." (We double-checked Kathy's story... every word of it was true.)

I reached out and hugged Kathy and she cried in my arms for a long time. It was tough getting my arms around her, because she just wouldn't put the paint can down. But she didn't seem to mind. I know I didn't....

I saw Kathy again, a couple of hours ago, eating dinner in our cafeteria. She made a point to come up and say hi. I made a point to give her an extra hug....

I've felt like crying tonight. I can't seem to stop feeling this way. I guess this story – the whole horrible, sad, unreal mess-has gotten to me tonight.

I guess that's why I just had to write you this letter.

Maybe things aren't so unfair in my life after all. Maybe I can move on and do something significant with what I have left. Things don't look quit so bad. So I think I'll just shut the party down, the self pity party that is and be thankful for what I have.

After looking back on my conversation with ('I') there are probably three problematic areas for him… me, myself and I.

Many times our wants come out of an unsettled, unsatisfied and restless soul.

St. Augustine a 4th century church father helps put this in perspective for us;

"Thou has formed us for Thyself,
and our hearts are restless
till they find rest in Thee."

Again, St. Augustine helps us define the problematic areas of our living.

"There can only be two basic loves,
the love of God unto the forgetfulness
of self,
or
the love of self unto the forgetfulness
of God."

"What one does not long for can be the object of neither despair nor hope."

St. Augustine

Chapter Six

DIRECTION

'N' started his second cup of coffee before he could get to the real reason and issue as to why we were here. It didn't take long to get through the small talk and now we were down to the wire for the reality check.

"I feel so lost, out of sync, I can't seem to get back on track. I don't know what to do next. I try this for awhile and then I'll try something else trying to find my self and nothing seems to work. I need help. I need direction."

I thought for a moment before answering then a story came to my mind. An artist once drew a picture. It represented a night-scene.

A solitary man is rowing a little skiff across a lake; the wind is high and stormy, the billows, white and crested, rage around his frail bark; and not a star, save one, that shines through the dark and angry sky above. Upon that lone star the voyager fixes his eyes, and keeps rowing away ...on, on, on through the midnight storm.

Written beneath the picture were these words,

"If I lose that I'm lost!"

William James once said, "That which holds our attention determines our direction."

I'm beginning to think that we are more easily distracted than we'd like to believe. Things, stuff pulls our focus away from important things. It takes just a moment of distraction for our lives to change forever. You take your eyes off the road for just a moment, the sound of bending steel and braking glass, now every things change forever.

You meet someone. You didn't plan it but you just looked away for a moment and now you look at your wife and children and nothing looks the same anymore. You've just discovered that infidelity isn't just a feeling it's a choice and the wrong one. You just didn't think it through.

Bernard Baruch once said, "Whatever failures I have known, whatever errors I have committed, whatever follies I have witnessed in private and public life, have been the consequences of action without thought."

Action with out thought will change everything.

Then we ask ourselves the formidable, dreadful and frightening questions?

What changed us?

What made us loose our focus?

How did we change direction in mid stream?

When things loose value and importance it's easy to get distracted.

I remember my dad singing a song of which I can only remember one line. It went like this; "Keep you hand upon the throttle and your eye upon the rail." It went along with him saying; "pay attention."

Distractions come in many shapes and sizes. Changes in direction can come through people and objects. Sometimes it's not big things that change our direction, sometimes its small things. A man of wealth was once ask; "how much money was enough" he answered; "just a little more." It's usually not the first or the last drink that does you end, it's all the drinks in between that eventually that brings you to that last glass. It's usually not the first puff of marijuana or the last line of cocaine, it's all the other recreational drugs in between that gets you to the last dose. It's the old saying; *"The straw that broke the camels back."*

It's dealing with things that change your direction, the subtle things. That's the rub. At first it was just a degree of change, all most imperceptible. But at the end, when you woke up, you were so far off that you couldn't see your way back.

Lillian Smith put this in perspective for us from her book *'Killers of the Dream'*;

"If only we could afford this zigzagging walk into the future! But each day the slowness becomes more dangerous. What will quicken us? What will illumine our minds? What can be said or done that will compel us to slough off inertia and complacency and take our stand for the human being against his unnumbered enemies? If only we could see the brokenness in each of us and the necessity for relationships; if we could realize our talent for bridging chasms that have always been and always will be. If only we could rise up against the killers of man's dream.

But, sometimes, that killer of dreams is in us and we do not know how to rid ourselves of it."

There for most of us is the culprit of our demise, our distraction and the responsible one for the change of direction. That distracter, the killer of the dream is in us and we must deal with him or her.

Oscar Wilde was by all estimates a literary genius and still today in many literary circles is considered so.

His life at the end spiraled out of control with such debauchery that he had to leave England. His best known work was the novel 'The Picture of Dorian Gray' which I believe to be, if you'll pardon the pun, a self-portrait and not on my list of books to read.

His decline is best stated in his own words:

"I started with almost everything in life that a young man would want. I let myself be lured into long spells of senseless and sensual ease... I became the spendthrift of my own genius... and to waste an eternal youth gave me curious joy... Tired of being on the heights, I deliberately went to the depths in search of a new sensation... What paradox was to me in the sphere of thought, perversity became to me in the sphere of passion. Desire at the end was a malady, a madness, or both. I grew careless of the lives of others. I took pleasure where it pleased me and passed on... I forgot that every little action of the common day makes or unmakes character. I ceased to be Lord over myself. I was no longer the captain of my soul and did not know it. I allowed pleasure to dominate me. I ended in horrible disgrace. There is only one thing for me now; absolute humility."

In conclusion he said that it was; 'foolhardy to try to obtain by one means what God had intended to be obtained by another.' In the end Oscar Wilde lost his family, his fortune, his self-respect and his will to live. He died bankrupt and broken at age 46.

I think that Oscar Wilde felt like the man in the John Eldredge book *'Wild at Heart'* when he said: "I don't know when I died, but I feel like I'm just using up oxygen."

If you lose direction, you'll become lost in a maze that will make you feel inexorably, inevitably confused and an overwhelming feeling of inescapable terror will inundate every fiber of your being. The only thing you'll be able to hear is the daunting scream of your own unrequited agony and it will deafen you to everything else... except... a still small voice... saying:

Matthew 11:28 through Matthew 11:30 (KJV) [28]Come unto me, all *ye* that labour and are heavy laden, and I will give you rest. [29]Take my yoke upon you, and learn of me; for I am meek and lowly in heart: and ye shall find rest unto your souls. [30]For my yoke *is* easy, and my burden is light.

Jesus Christ

There are things in our personal past history that while we were engaging them, while we were doing them in varying degrees they seemed harmless, innocent and we had no fear. Then life took on meaning and when we looked back at our past, it made us fearful of our future. At that moment our history began to produce a seed that if not dealt with would have a harvest in our future.

We had our own mantra, our own tune, *"I did it my way, It's my life."* Somehow that seems frightening to think I'm making the choices for my direction on my own.

That's the horror or our nature... it's in the not knowing.

In the work *Theologia Germanica*, discovered and published by Martin Luther 1516 puts this thought into perspective for us:

"Since the life of Christ *is every way most bitter to nature...* and the Self... and the Me... (for in the true life of Christ, the Self and the Me and nature must be forsaken and lost and die altogether), therefore in each of us, *nature hath a horror of it.*"

Theologia Germanica, XX

I know what 'N' was talking about, when he said he felt out of sync and out of touch. There have been times I have felt completely off the grid. There seemed to be no way to track where I'd been or where I was going. The only way I knew I had a past was the pressing memories that kept repeating and punctuating themselves in my mind with an exclamation mark. They seemed to be, only the memories that I didn't want and when they came I wanted to be so far off the grid that even they couldn't find me. That however is never the case.

Nothing obliterates the selective memory that has developed on its own. It didn't just happen on its own. I had nursed this seed that I planted and now it was giving birth. I was reaping a harvest.

Brennan Manning said it best; *"What is denied cannot be healed."* Nothing can hide from this insidious monster. It lurks in the darkened canyons of our soul and if not dealt with, it will deal with you. You can't bury it in success, promotions, accolades, pats on the back for achievements or hide under the influence of presupposed elixirs, pacifiers or placebos. To disconnect, to disable and to disarm this terrible, relentless and unquenchable pain... there is only one place to go, To Christ, to Calvary, to the Cross. It is only there that this killer, this purveyor death can be swallowed up in life.

Malcolm Muggeridge, one of England's most articulate journalists, and sums up his pursuit of pleasure.

"I may, I suppose, regard myself, or pass for being, as a relatively successful man. People occasionally stare at me in the streets – that's fame. I can fairly easily earn enough to qualify for admission to the higher slopes of the Internal Revenue – that's success.

Furnished with money and a little fame even the elderly, if they care to, may partake of trendy diversions – that's pleasure. It might happen once in a while that something I said or wrote was sufficiently heeded for me to persuade myself that it represented a serious impact on our time – that's fulfillment.

Yet I say to you – and I beg you to believe me – multiply these tiny triumphs by a million, add them all together, and they are nothing – less than nothing, a positive impediment – measured against one draught of that living water Christ offers to the spiritually thirsty, irrespective of who or what they are."

Bertrand Russell, a noted atheist, wrote that he could not live as though ethical values were simple a matter *'of personal taste, and that he therefore found his own views 'incredible'*. *"I do not know the solution."* Russell's conclusion of the matter; *"we must build our lives upon the firm foundation of unyielding despair."*

In physics, *'entropy'* means that anything left to its self will eventually disintegrate until it reaches its most elemental form. When I'm stripped of all of me, there's not much left. If I let the world of darkness win me over… it will drag me under. If I'm left to my own devices, to rely on my own design, then I'm afraid the house will fall. Sand for a foundation doesn't make for a firm footing. So if that's my hope, if that's all that's left then I am standing on *'the firm foundation of unyielding despair.'*

1 Corinthians 15:54 (KJV) [54]...Death is swallowed up in victory.

The Apostle Paul

"Make me wise to see all things today under the form of eternity, and make me brave to face all the changes in my life which such a vision may entail: through the grace of Christ my Saviour. Amen"

John Baillie
Scottish theologian (1886 – 1960)

Chapter Seven

REFLECTIONS IN THE MIRROR

In looking back at all this people I dealt with in my life time I realized they were all a part of me. What has frightened me in my discovery is how much intentional ignorance was pervasive in much of what was happening to me. And since I am now aware that every person I meet is not a mere mortal, but an immoral being I must be reticent of my actions, conduct and my speech.

We have a connection. We are not alone.

He is the only security for one such as my self and others like me who has wandered down the road of life sometimes secure and sometimes not so secure. A willing surrender to Him, a thought out choice that says; "Without reservation, yes I will give who and whatever I am to Christ." He is the assurance from the center to the circumference of our lives I believe then and only then, will a new sense of hope, dispelling fear will arise and give you a new direction for you life.

Let us finish better than we started. Let us not end with regrets and memories full of disappointment and failures.

Ravi Zacharais in his book *'Cries Of The Heart'* relates to us of the French author Guy de Maupassant whose life spelled heartache. Maupassant was one of the great writers of short stories. During the 1880s Maupassant created some 300 short stories, six novels. Within ten years he rose from obscurity to fame and fortune. His material obsessions spoke volumes of a life of affluence, a yacht, a house on the Coast, a flat in Paris. Critics praised him, men admired him, and women worshiped him. Yet at the height of his fame he went insane, a condition brought on, many believe, by a sexually transmitted disease. On New Year's Day in 1892, he tried to cut his throat with a letter opener, and he lived out the last weeks of his life in a private asylum on the

French Riviera. After weeks and months of mindless utterances and debilitating pain, he died at the age of forty-two. De Maupassant penned his own epitaph: *"I have coveted everything and taken pleasure in nothing."*

It is the words of Christ that resound in our ears for time and eternity. It demands a conclusion, an answer to your value system;

"For what shall it profit a man, if he shall gain the whole world, and lose his own soul?" Mark 8:36 (KJV)

Shakespeare lays the problem where it belongs; *"Men at some time are masters of their fates: The fault, dear Brutus, is not in our stars, but in ourselves..."* (Julius Caesar – Act I, Scene II).

Again Shakespeare in Hamlet Prince of Denmark; *"I am very proud, revengeful, ambitious; with more offences at my beck – than I have thoughts to put them in, imagination to give them shape, or time to act them in..."*

Here for many of us lies the unscrupulous nature lying in the belly of the beast. It's appetite insatiable, voracious, devouring eventually our own lives from the inside out.

"The fault, dear Brutus, is not in our stars, but in ourselves..." Much of our inability to exchange hopelessness and helplessness for hope and help is; *"I am very proud"* Hamlet said. My mother used a scripture many times reminding me to walk carefully.

Proverbs 16:18 (KJV) [18]Pride *goeth* before destruction, and an haughty spirit before a fall.

I am always challenged when I read the poem *'Invictus'* by William Ernest Henley.

Out of the night that covers me,
Black as the pit from pole to pole.
I thank whatever gods may be
For my unconquerable soul.

In the fell clutch of circumstance,
I have not winced nor cried aloud,
Under the bludgeoning of chance,
My head is bloody, but unbowed

It matters not how strait the gate,
How charged with punishment the scroll

I am the master of my fate,
I am the captain of my soul.

If I'm the captain of my soul, I could be on a ship of fools. What is that old saying; *"if a man becomes his own lawyer, he has a fool for a client."*

If there is *'Chaos'* in our lives it can only be *'Conquered'* by the *'Prince Of Peace.'* Only He can stand on the deck of our embattled ship, embroiled in the heated exchange of life being fired at us from all sides at point bland range. Only He can speak peace to the crippling, debilitating storm that has darkened our souls with clouds of past pain, present hurts and the anticipated ugliness of what the future holds if the past is repeated. Only He can step in to the emotionally tangled web of frustrations and separate the hanging, lifeless unnumbered threads of our lives. Only He, the *Christ of the Crisis'* can step into the bankrupt and condemned property that we call life and redeem it.

Fanny Jane Crosby who wrote thousands of poems and hymns though she was blind came to know the *'Christ of the Crisis'* in 1850. One of the great hymns Fanny Crosby wrote *'Re-deemed,'* my mother used to sing. I can hear them singing at this moment as I reflect back over my life;

Re-deemed how I love to proclaim it!
Re-deemed by the blood of the lamb;
Re-deemed thro' His infinite mercy,
His child, and forever, I am

Then my dad would follow with another Fanny Crosby song;

Verse
Blessed assurance, Jesus is mine!
O, what a foretaste of glory divine!
Heir of salvation, purchase of God,
Born of His Spirit, washed in His blood.

Chorus
This is my story, This is my song,
Praising my Savior all the day long;

For many of us the *'Reflections in the Mirror'* are like going to a carnival and passing in front of the mirror that distorts our image, making us look crooked and bent. We feel like the *Hunchback of Notre Dame, The Phantom of the Opera,* or the beast in the *Beauty and the Beast.* Inside where it always hurts the most, the place that's covered by the mask we wear, not all of us, but some of us, and believe me I know, that's where *we* or at least *(I)* felt like the *Hunchback, the Phantom and the Beast*. I know I've played this song before, but I know the words and the melody by heart. It wasn't the *Mask of Zorro* I wore it was a mask to cover the distortions of the ruined master piece, that the artist had not intended. I wasn't the artist that could paint a new life. I could only paint with the colors, dark colors that only pain from a wounded soul can create

The nineteenth-century American writer Nathaniel Hawthorne offered this insight: *"No man can for any considerable time, wear one face to himself and another to the multitude without finally getting bewildered as to which is the true one."*

Confusion reigned.

However when we look into the eyes of our Redeemer a metamorphous takes place and our image is transformed before us. The first images we see become the pierced hands, the riven side and the crown of thorns. From then on we will never look the same again.

The image of *The Phantom of the Opera, The Hunchback of Notre Dame and the Beast* is gone and has been replace with something originally intended. The image of the lost, now found. The image of the blind now with sight, the image of the insignificant made significant. Christ seems to have great interest in *The Least, The Last and The Lost* of which I can say like the Apostle Paul *"I am the chief."* It is not in a false sense of humility that I profess to be the least, the last and the lost, all of us without Christ, were lost. It's just that I was. In my own mind I felt like the least and the last. One thing, that was for sure, is the fact that I was lost but now thank God, I'm found.

So in the midst of a chaotic storm He can speak peace and calm can come. He can *Conquer Chaos*. The words to the Apostle Paul still rings true, *"My Grace is sufficient."*

Grace really is Amazing and it's free.

WITHOUT HUMANITIES:

Approval-Christ is still the answer.
Validation-He is still the truth personified.
Affirmation-He is still master of the storm.
Respect-He is still Lord over all.
Help-He still maintains the universe.

We are still sheep and He is still the
Great Shepherd.

Healing of the Bruised

Bruised, feeling rejected and refused
Hurts not fleeting, but somehow confused
It's not the breaking of a bone
But tis the thought of being alone

Not the bleeding for anyone to see
Just the color of the soul that cannot be free
From the pain of words, not spoken in Love
Oh for the wings to soar so far above

I cannot deny, nor live in a lie
The bruise of the heart that I cannot hide
Oh perilous journey without cloak or shield
Not even a sword that I might wield

So I close my eyes that I might lose
The ability to see and hence refuse
The toil of this labor, my brow
covered in sweat
Then comes the knowing that there is hope
for me yet

Your hand grasping mine with such
delicate grace
Your arms around me, what sweet embrace
The sound of your voice with
the hope of life
The touch of your breath removes the strife

The bruises will heal

Printed in the United States
60127LVS00002BA/223-510